GESUNDHEIT, DUMMY!

The Best of Baloo

Gesundheit, Dummy!

The Best of Baloo

Rex May

JoNa Books
Bedford, Indiana

Copyright 2000 by Rex May
All rights reserved. Printed in the U.S.A.

No part of this publication may be reproduced or transmitted in any
form or by any means. Electrical or mechanical, including photocopy,
recording, or any storage information and retrieval system, now
known or to be invented, without permission in writing from the pub-
lisher.

ISBN: 0-9657929-3-5

Library of Congress Number: 99-071530

1st printing April 2000

To Jean:
Wife
Mother
Muse
Business Manager
Model of models

"Because Daddy doesn't want to draw Garfield!"

"I don't think Rush Limbaugh is laughing at you."

"Hey, don't think of it as welfare — think of it as 'shirkers' compensation.'"

"Oh, nothing in particular — I'm just here to curry favor."

"I did have a job once, sir, but it was too labor-intensive."

"You'll be able to lead a normal life — except, of course, for your enormous medical bills."

"Thank you, sir — you may now pick up the pieces and get on with your life."

"Oh, jury selection will be easy — there are <u>lots</u> of volunteers."

"Every time I go on an ego trip, I'm hijacked by terrorists."

"I have the right to comprehensive health care, and you make me sick!"

"He says he's looking for an honest man — shall we book him on suspicion?"

Congress

"Ha, ha! That's a scream! — Let me tell you one of <u>my</u> campaign promises."

"You have to admire his candor!"

"Gesundheit, Mom."

"He's the best manure-shoveller I've ever had, and he's quitting next week to go into politics."

"Improved service, expanded window hours, better public relations . . . I <u>hate</u> breaking in a new Postmaster General."

"This isn't <u>either</u> a free country!"

CONGRESS

"Hey, don't knock poverty programs — they can be <u>very</u> lucrative."

I'd rather be right than President, but I don't <u>insist</u> on it."

"Not <u>too</u> speedy a trial — I haven't thought up an alibi yet!"

"You can't let private charities take over welfare, Your Majesty —
You wiped them all out with your last tax hike."

"How do I go about getting a non-working number?"

"How was <u>I</u> to know Perry Mason would make a comeback?"

"'Speak? — I'd really prefer to <u>fax</u>."

"I tried to put her on a pedestal, and she got up on a soap box."

"That's nothing — wait till I tell you what _my_ wife did."

"I've been busy, too — I made doilies for all the stalagmites."

"Grandchildren visiting again, Pomeroy?"

"It's for you."

"A Congressman, eh? — I'll give you fifteen bucks for your soul, tops."

"Wouldn't you know it? — I sliced it right into Purgatory!"

"Would you believe, it was my evil twin?"

"The prisons are full, so I'll just have the City Engineers tear up the street in front of your house."

"You can trim the budget a little more, Sire — the prisoners in the dungeon have gone on a hunger strike."

"Was that a spiritual insight, or just awkwardness?"

CHURCH AND STATE KEEP-AWAY

"One thing about being broke and unemployed — it's recession-proof."

"It's funny — as soon as I got elected, my kleptomania cleared up."

"To begin with, my son, everything is illusory . . . Hey! — you gave me counterfeit money."

"Mobster'? — I thought I was agreeing to testify against a <u>lobster!</u>"

"You killed eight people? — I fed the bears in a National Park!"

"In an effort to 'level the playing field,' the Government today decided to tax everybody at 100%. . ."

"Whenever politicians start talking about a new deal, you can be sure that the cards are marked."

"I called your office today, and they said you retired three years ago."

"This 'nuclear winter' thing — how will it affect <u>Christmas?</u>"

"Never mind the meaning of life — just tell me how to get out of Tibet!"

"You forgot your hat? Look, kid — excuses don't cut it in this business!"

"It's your husband, Ma'am — he was shot while attempting to conceal income."

"We've completed that study you ordered on the private sector, Sire — The only things left are two shoe-shine boys and a hot dog stand."

"You amnesiacs never learn, do you?"

"It started as a referendum, and ended up as a recall."

"I've checked out all your options, Mr. Fogarty, and it looks like your only way out is to get a job somewhere."

"Money may not be everything, but it sure is <u>versatile.</u>"

No thanks — I'm trying to quit."

"Think about it — if you were a Congressman, would <u>you</u> want more prison space available?"

"Bad news, Sire — it's Mongrel Hordes!"

"If this is a democracy, how come <u>voters</u> don't get matching funds?"

"We're a little shorthanded out here today, guys — anybody want to do some jury duty?"

"They expect us to vote <u>cold sober</u>?"

"If bribing a Congressman isn't a legitimate business expense, what <u>would</u> be?"

"Of course there's a record turnout — You never let anybody vote before!"

"I'm from the City Zoning Commission, sir — I'm afraid that mustache will have to go."

Congress

"And I thought I was corrupt!"

"Oh, you poor man — the Democrats are going to nominate you for President!"

"Scram! — I don't endorse candidates!"

"My professional consulting fee is $300, but I can give you some harebrained ideas for $50 apiece."

"Be specific, Miss Myers — which Napoleon is here?"

"If you can't say anything good about a person, you're probably my mother-in-law."

"I won't be here for a few days, sir — I'm attending a fund-raising seminar."

"My client did <u>not</u> escape, Your Honor — his prison was so crowded, somebody pushed him out the window."

"Clever defense, but I can't buy calling insider trading an alternate lifestyle."

"Shh, wait! — I'm getting an astral message from Freud!"

"President Clinton and Senator Kennedy today announced a joint plan to get more women into government."

"This 'infrastructure' you keep talking about — does it have anything to do with vegetables?"

"It'll help the ecology <u>and</u> the economy, Mr. President — biodegradable money!"

"Due to the theatrical nature of politics lately, 'Crossfire' will now merge with 'Entertainment Tonight'"

"Nobody takes you seriously? — Are you trying to be funny?"

"I have to flunk a few things, Dad, so I'll qualify for a government grant to go to college."

"Did you bring foreign aid this time?"

"You're not here to provide famine relief, eh? — That's what you think!"

"I try to run the family like a democracy, but what I really need is a line-item veto."

"Oh, I go to college — what do you do for a living?"

"You think it's <u>easy</u> spending your money faster than you can make it?"

"Just money, sir — my union won't allow me to accept food."

"You no-good bum! — you just sprained my wrist!"

"You're <u>sure</u> the other driver was a crash-test dummy?"

"Actually, if Polly has any choice in the matter, Polly would prefer a burger and fries."

"By George, I think you're right — Old Shep <u>is</u> trying to tell us something!"

"You think <u>you</u> have a hard life? — I have to listen to <u>crazy</u> people all day!"

"Of course my foreign policy is incomprehensible — it's <u>foreign</u>!"

"No thanks — I hate to eat and run."

"Elections are easier to take if you think of them as performance art."

"I got 75 years — I was driving under the influence, and ran over a spotted owl."

"It's more traditional and American than the 'Star Wars' system, General — I call it it 'Gone With The Wind.'"

"Really? — I was the first one in <u>my</u> family to graduate from college, too!"

"Sure, the food is lousy — but we get pure mountain spring water to drink!"

"Can you adapt to unusual situations?"

"Did you hear about Knoedelbaum? — He developed an immortality pill and choked to death on it."

"I hope you're satisfied — I turned down a chance to trade him for a brand new dollhouse!"

"Grrrr . . ."

"Talk about a great lawyer — he plea bargained me into a job with the city!"

"Hey! — You're rubbing your greasy hair all over my nice clean wall!"

"'It's a Wonderful Life' will not be seen tonight, so that we may bring you a special Presidential address . . ."

"I call it a 'bug-zapper.'"

BEWARE

"My psychiatrist told me to take up a hobby, so I became a psychiatrist."

"I'm not really homeless — I'll go home as soon as my mother-in-law's visit is over."

"Gesundheit."

For original artwork, or complete catalog of books:

JoNa Books
P. O. Box 336
Bedford, IN 47421
jonabook @kiva.net
http://www.kiva.net/~jonabook